FRENCH UNDRESSING

NAUGHTY POSTCARDS FROM 1900 TO 1920

FRENCH UNDRESSING

BY
PAUL
HAMMOND

JUPITER BOOKS · LONDON

BY THE SAME AUTHOR
Marvellous Méliès, London, 1974

The author and publishers would like to thank
the Ellis Postcard Collection without which
this volume would not have been possible.
Additionally, the author wishes to thank
Valerie Monahan, Patrick Hughes, Mike Wallington,
and Chris.

First published in 1976 by
JUPITER BOOKS (LONDON) LIMITED
167 Hermitage Road, London N4 1LZ

SBN 904041 40 9

Produced by Forrester & Archer, London.
Set on the Monophoto in 12/14pt Century Schoolbook 227
by V. Siviter Smith & Company Limited, Birmingham

PRINTED BY HAZELL WATSON & VINEY LTD, AYLESBURY, BUCKS

CONTENTS

INTRODUCTION

Something SPECIAL, Sir?

A Parisian *passage.*
You could rely on finding
naughty postcards here.

People haven't always seen a lot in popular art. The poet Arthur
Rimbaud was one of the first who did. In 1873 he announced the
dawn of this new kind of sensibility in his prose poem *Alchemy
of the Word.* "I liked," the 19 year-old poet wrote, "stupid paintings,
door panels, stage sets, backdrops for acrobats, signs, popular
engravings, old-fashioned literature, church Latin, erotic books
with bad spelling, novels of our grandmothers, fairy tales, little
books from childhood, old operas, ridiculous refrains, naive
rhythms." Rimbaud recognised that even the most unsophisticated
and traditional forms of art could have an irrational, hypnotic
fascination for the person intelligent enough to open his eyes
to them. Had the picture postcard been invented when Rimbaud
wrote his poem he would undoubtedly have included it in his
inventory of "popular art", and it is not impossible that one specific
kind of card – the erotic kind – would have appealed to him more
than any other.

The "art" of the postcard lies in its basically artless exploration
of the unusual, in its freedom of thought and expression, and
in its eroticism. A modern sexologist has said that "eroticism
reigns when it is a question of suggestion, of allusion, of expectation even to the point of obsession" (J.-M. Lo Duca). In contrast
to this "when the genitals are exhibited obscenely – and not symbo-
lically or decoratively – we enter the closed, sadly limited world
of pornography." By that definition the postcards in this collection
are placed firmly within the domain of eroticism, not pornography.
(Anyway, the distinction between eroticism and pornography – the
latter is not without its delights, of course – is as much one of
aesthetics, even of lighting and "focus", as of the content of the
image.)

7

So the erotic emphasis is on symbolism. A sexologist of the postcard era, Havelock Ellis, defined erotic symbolism as the tendency whereby sexual attraction is focused, or displaced, onto some special part of the body (the foot, say), on some inanimate object (stockings, perhaps), or in the form of certain specialised acts (whipping, maybe). Fetishism is part and parcel of all this. The virtue of erotic symbolism (a tendency Ellis stressed was perfectly normal) was that it involved "not only the play of fancy and imagination . . . but also a certain amount of power of concentrating the attention on a point outside the natural path of instinct and the ability to form new mental constructions around that point." Symbolism, then, signifies fluidity of imagination.

Since the Renaissance artists have used pictorial symbolism, not in an unconscious way as some writers would have us believe, but specifically to suggest erotic ideas to the onlooker. Lucas Cranach is a good example here. Later, too, the witty and calculated use of symbolism became an invaluable weapon in the new language of caricature, which flourished as the popular print. By the beginning of the 19th century we find an artist like Thomas Rowlandson using a splendid array of visual *double entendres* (cannons, swords, flutes) as well as more subtle and playful erotic symbols (a clarinet lying across an open book, tumescent teapots, and so on) in his lithographs. It was this highly spirited tradition of excess that the picture postcard inherited.

In art, as in life, it is context that can charge an object, that can give it vitality as a symbol. Context can give a commonplace accessory, one that appears to have a merely decorative, anecdotal function, an exaggerated significance. Illustrations (141) to (145) are a case in point. They show a naked girl opening a window, picking up a watering can, and watering some potted plants. Given the context of her bare body, the abundant flowers, the watering can, even the window frames, take on a more than "normal" significance: they are eroticised–they may even be symbols. Context is vital, too, in other forms, like the pun and the *double entendre*. In a card like the one in the *Parisian Curiosities* series (149), where a girl sits astride the dome of Sacré-Coeur, the joke is entirely dependent on the juxtaposition of the legs and the cathedral dome. In this context Sacré-Coeur is not quite so sacred! It just so happened that as Freud, and other sexologists of the period like Krafft-Ebing, Moll, and Ellis, were building their theories of sexual symbolism the lowly picture postcard was merrily and consciously proposing its pictorial usage.

The history of the postcard, as a variety of stationery, has been ably described in books by Richard Carline, C. W. Hill, Tonie and Valmai Holt, and Ado Kyrou. These, basically, are the facts:

The golden age of the picture postcard we are used to sending stretches from 1900 to 1920, but its origins are older than that. In the form of a plain, pre-stamped correspondence card the postcard was suggested first by Dr. Heinrich von Stephan at a German postal congress in 1865. His proposal aroused no interest. Four years later Dr. Emmanuel Herrmann, an Austrian professor, revived the idea, and this time it was taken up by the Austrian government, which introduced its *Correspondenz-Karte* in 1869. One side of the straw-coloured card was for the name and address, the other was for the message. In 1870 the governments of Great Britain and France followed suit, and in 1873 the USA did likewise. In 1875 the General Postal Union was founded–thanks largely to the efforts of von Stephan who was by now the General Post Director of the North German Confederation–its aim being to facilitate the international transportation of mail. To do this standardised size and postal rate were necessary: the postcard was to be $5\frac{1}{2}$ by $3\frac{1}{2}$ inches, and cost a penny to send anywhere within the Union.

By the 1880s line engravings of views had begun to intrude onto the previously blank correspondence side of the card. This meant shorter messages: there was less room to write in, and the pictured view meant you didn't have to expend words describing it. The Paris Exhibition of 1889 really launched picture postcards. It became the thing to ascend the spanking new Eiffel Tower and post a card from the top. The vogue for ascents, with "X" marking the spot, had begun. By 1899 the European industry was expanding rapidly. Great Britain, with 38.5M inhabitants, produced 14M cards; Germany with 50M people, turned out 88M; France, with a population of 38M, produced 8M cards; and Belgium, with 6.2M people, produced 12M cards. The 1900 Exhibition in Paris coincided with the début of the golden age. Until then the price of cards was high, due to the expensive production processes of drypoint, etching and lithography that were used. The invention of photolithography, the collotype, rotary printing and chromolithography, c. 1900, meant cheaper cards. And it meant that the image could come into its own. In 1902 the "divided back" card was introduced in Great Britain. One side of the card was completely covered by an image; the other side was divided in half, one half for the address, the other for correspondence. By 1904 France followed suit, then came Germany in 1905 and the USA in 1907. The industry was booming. By 1914 twenty cards were mailed annually for every British man, woman and child. On top of this were the millions bought and put straight into albums. The First World War saw some lowering of standards, in content and in quality, for the best produced cards came from Germany. In 1918 the decline was quickened, in Great Britain at least, by the doubling of the postal rate, the first increase since 1870.

"Cartophilia" (collecting postcards) was a craze that swept through Europe at the same time as postcards did. Another name for it was "cartomania": you could be a maniac for postcards as you could be a maniac for music (a melomaniac), or a maniac for breaking wind artfully (a petomaniac–"Le Petomane" was a music-hall artiste who did just that). To begin with cards were used and collected by those wealthy enough to travel and hence be able to secure them, but by 1910 the postcard had become a product for the masses and cards were collected by everybody. Collectors' clubs publishing specialised journals that announced forthcoming cards and gave advice and criticism had appeared by 1900; journals like *The Picture Postcard Magazine of Travel, Philately and Art* (London), *La Diane* and *Mes Cartes postales* (both Paris). One of their functions was to propose classifications for the cartophile, and one such category–which describes the cards in this book–was the "French" card (hence *French Undressing*).

Even as early as 1900 France was famous for its libidinous visual exports, and Paris was synonymous with the image of decadence. Every young man of means and "artistic" temperament dreamed of going there to "complete" his education. Richard Carline claims that the trade in French cards, and similar pin-up kinds, was a way of shattering the virtual monopoly women held in the world of cartophilia, and of opening up postcard collecting for men. The album was the repository for the French card (as for all others). Such erotic albums were midway between an art gallery and a book, and secrecy lent them a ritual value far greater than the albums of views that were part of contemporary drawing-room furniture.

During their heyday postcards could be bought everywhere, in hotel lobbies, railway stations, restaurants, libraries, and from newsvendors' kiosks. It is difficult to know exactly who sold French cards–the information was not openly proffered–but one place has become synonymous with them, the Parisian *passage*. These arcades, which connected the great boulevards in the city centre, housed souvenir shops, wax museums, small theatres, the offices of the first film companies and, presumably, postcard dealers. Louis Aragon described one such arcade, the Passage de l'Opéra, in his novel *Paris Peasant* (1926). The book is set later than the French card days, but the exoticism of the place is well portrayed by the surrealist writer, who regarded it as the locus of certain modern "myths". Aragon's passage evokes the image of Soho: here are lodging houses, a café, bookshops, a philatelist's, strip joints, a bath house, and a truss specialist's. An idea of the kind of place this was–where you used to be able to buy erotic postcards–is given by an establishment Paul Valéry once described to the novelist: "an agency which accepted unstamped letters and arranged to have them posted from any desired point of the globe to the address written on the envelope, a facility that would allow the customer to feign a voyage to the far east, for example, without moving an inch from the far west of some secret adventure."

For the collector who could not travel to the French capital for his cards magazines like *Rabelais* offered a mail order service. An advertisement in an issue of 1902 offers "Suggestive Postcards for Art Lovers and Collectors", of sets like "Ardent Kisses", "The Cigarette", "In the Corn", "Alone At Last", and "Butterfly Hunting". They could be had in black-and-white or hand-tinted, with little difference in price (black-and-white cards cost 18 centimes each; coloured ones cost 21 centimes).

Such *risqué* pictures were bound to fall foul of the powers that were. In 1891 Senator René Bérenger had launched an appeal for the setting up of a "Central Society For Protest Against Licence in the Streets". Month after month this good man, the Lord Longford of his day, bombarded the French Senate with legislative proposals for censoring the salacious and witty lyrics to be heard in every *café-concert* and the saucy printed matter to be seen displayed in every newsvendor's kiosk. Bérenger had some success. For example, he made the wearing of the *maillot*, a flesh coloured body-stocking, obligatory in the theatre, where naked ladies were wont to perform. His efforts extended to the erotic postcard. On August 22 1900 the *gendarmerie* raided shops all over Paris and seized 80,000 "objectionable" cards. It was to be the first of many such raids. And the *maillot* made its appearance in the postcard, both actually and in a simulated way (by retouching).

Who produced our cards? Many of the photographic ones are anonymous, the combined work of unknown models, scenery painters, photographers, retouchers and colourists. By 1910 there were 33,000 people working in the French postcard industry. Even when signed (presumably by the photographer) there is little to differentiate one card from another. Anonymity was the rule: the artisans involved did not consider themselves artists, and never signed their work; furthermore, it was safer not to let on you'd produced the card, this made prosecution difficult. Nevertheless, during the 1914–18 War, when the French card had become more acceptable–the cards cheered up the soldiers at the front–companies and sometimes photographers signed their product.

The graphic, drawn cards, then as now eagerly collected, were usually signed by the artists, many of whom worked in the field of magazine illustration and poster design. Examples of their work were paraded in luxurious magazines like *La Vie Parisienne*, *Le Journal amusant*, *Le Fétard*, *La Vie en rose* and *Rabelais*. They include Alphonse Mucha, Raphael Kirchner, Xavier Sager, Suzanne Meunier, Hérouard, Maurice Millière, H. Gerbault and Léonnec. There is a lower stratum of the graphic card, which employs erotic puns and *double entendres* in a rather literary way. Often anonymous, for the jokes are usually older than the illustrator, who could hardly claim paternity, the best artist in this field was Fox.

Most of the photographic postcards in *French Undressing* are closely related in both subject and conventions to contemporary academic painting, to the kind of art exhibited in the Paris Salon and the Royal Academy in London. It is usual for a new medium to look to an older one for inspiration and legitimacy. The artisans who made postcards looked to Fine Art. The typical Salon painting, by Gérôme, Bouguereau, Courtois, or Chocarne-Moreau, was created on a "heroic" scale, photographically painted, and dignified in subject matter. Historical, mythological or oriental subjects–anything that was far removed from everyday existence–were *de rigueur*, and were the pretext under which the female nude could appear. The scandal surrounding Manet's "Olympia" in 1863, which was considered to be of an insolent and obscene realism, had never been forgotten. Only unreal, idealised nudes were permitted: "no underarm or pubic hair, because this recalls our animal essence. No real scenes, because they would be sure to touch on the scabrous. The nude must be given a pretext of antiquity, of heroism, or must be illuminated by the Bengal lights of the fairy story or allegory." (Patrick Waldberg).

11

Just as the literary *salon* had given way to the café as the breeding ground of art, so Salon painting gave way to the picture postcard. The great achievement of the latter is that, in appropriating the conventions of academic art, the postcard destroys its bogus authority. A stepping stone in this process was the appearance around 1890 of photographic albums of nudes, like Emile Bayard's monthly journal *Le Nu esthétique* (which was prefaced by Gérôme and dedicated to Bouguereau), intended for the use of budding academicians. Meant as a prop for a particular kind of painting, albums like these unwittingly helped to undermine the mystique of that painting. They began a process of demystification that culminated in the erotic postcard. The eroticism in Salon painting was there, but never openly admitted. The postcard puts that eroticism in the limelight, so that it can't be missed.

It is true to say that "as the ancient myths and the lives of the heroes were not generally known and certainly not emotionally cogitated over by the public, the dramatic element of picture-making gradually faded away. All that was left for the picture-maker dramatist was a series of subjects that while apt to sloppy sentimentality were actually vapid and empty, because the pictures represented no one in particular. It is very difficult to arouse emotions about the human troubles and emotions of no one in particular" (William M. Ivins). The democratic erotic postcard is about *particular*, if stereotyped, people. No matter how unreal, how "academic" their surroundings, the men and women in these photographed cards have real faces and real bodies.

It has been said that photography and socialism were born simultaneously. In 1888 the most democratic of cameras, the Kodak, was put on the market. One result of putting photography within lots of people's reach was the development of unorthodox techniques. Soon, books of photographic amusements appeared, like Albert Hopkins' popular *Magic, Stage Illusions and Scientific Diversions, Including Trick Photography* (1897), and numerous articles about artifice in photography were published. These described techniques like retouching, drawing on the image, vignetting and airbrushing. They were to become part of the aesthetic of the picture postcard. In 1902 do-it-yourself postcards were introduced. All you had to do was stick a negative to a sensitised card (price 2d.), expose it to light, develop it in water, fix it in "hypo", and then dry it.

Next to all this was the use of photomontage and collage. O. G. Rejlander and H. P. Robinson had made composite photographs as early as the 1850s. The most popular postcard photomontages were of lots of babies. Fifteen years later the Dadaists and the Russian Constructivists appropriated this splendid medium. In the realm of collage all manner of things were stuck to cards: leather, feathers, tinsel, human hair, even glass eyes. Max Ettlinger was the doyen of the postcard collagists. He was producing his cards at the same time as the Cubists were "inventing" the art of collage.

Photographic portraiture had always taken place in the studio, using natural light, painted backcloths and a few real props. The *carte-de-visite*, a personalised giveaway token, is typical of this conception. It too became part of the postcard aesthetic.

It would be impossible to write a meaningful introductory essay describing the social context of the picture postcard for it is impossible to imagine that context today. We would be reaching after a mirage to try and do so. Even "objective" records like the photographs and movies of the period have taken on, with the passing of time, an unreal quality. Jean-Luc Godard was probably right when he said that the naturalistic films of Lumière did little to describe their era, but that the fantastic fairy tales of Méliès did a lot. How do picture postcards relate objectively to their social context? It's difficult to say. They may tell us that people made love, exploited each other, slept in beds, or that they went to war (so what's new?). What the cards describe are imaginings conditioned by certain aesthetic conventions which are conditioned in turn by practical matters like technology. Our French cards are imaginings about sexuality. That Paris should be the factory of such dreams has, of course, a relation to contemporary morality and to the city's traditional role as the producer of "luxury" commodities. But this is of little importance compared to the vitality of the postcards as images in their own right. The relation of these images to their social base is difficult to ascertain because we have no way of measuring it, as we have only an imperfect idea of that base, but as images with their own internal laws our postcards have particular meanings which may allude to other external ones. When this is the case we will mention them. In a word, our postcard images have life, their social context is dead.

It is usually the case that postcards are not reproduced in books in sets, although many were published in this form. One set will tell a simple story, subtitled by a written narrative–"The Actress' Dressing Room", (169) to (174) for instance. Another will have no narrative as such but will show five or six tableaux that are almost identical–the "Downstream" set, (196) to (200). In this the picture postcard bears some relation to the so-called "primitive" cinema, to the simple little films of Léon Gaumont, Charles Pathé, but above all Georges Méliès, and to the comic strip. Surely it isn't just coincidence that the last two media were invented at the same moment? The Lumière brothers' *Cinématographe* appeared in 1895; Richard Outcault's strip *The Yellow Kid* surfaced in 1896, Rudolph Dirks' *The Katzenjammer Kids* in 1897 (although both comics and films had been anticipated by other inventions throughout the 19th century).

Just as the discovery of perspective gave people a new point of view in the 15th century, four hundred years later they had begun to look at the world in a different way, they had started to read the world in little pieces. It was photography that brought about this change, for it permitted "bits" of reality to be recorded. (Muybridge and Marey worked on this problem). All that remained for artists to do was to put these bits back together again. The serialised postcard, with its standardised size, was part of this new way of seeing. Perhaps the sequential images of the *carte-de-visite* sets, popular since the 1850s, influenced the photographers working in postcard production. (The modern equivalent of the *cartes-de-visite* are the uncut sheets of exposures made in the self-operating booths you find in railway stations). One can imagine flicking though a set of our postcards and making the figures in them "move", as in the flicker books and *mutoscopes* ("What the Butler Saw" machines) popular at that time.

The films of Georges Méliès are the ones that come closest to the look and spirit of our postcards. An artisan himself (who, incidentally, ran his business from an office in the Passage de l'Opéra, the Mecca of the French cartophile), Méliès made 500 films between 1896 and 1912, ranging from one minute to half an hour in length. Like the postcard artisans' Méliès' productions were simple narratives, a chain of "effects" filmed by a stationary camera, before a painted backdrop, using a few real props. And like them Méliès was a specialist in eroticism, populating his pictures with angels and temptresses, with astral deities, butterfly-women, and fairies, with uncomplicated *femmes-fatale*. Like Pathé, whose "broad scenes of a piquant nature" had popular appeal, Méliès was a director of stag films. One of his briefest and best, *After the Ball* of 1897, has just the feeling of our postcard series. In it a lady wearing a *maillot* (played by Méliès' mistress) undresses in front of a backcloth representing a panelled room, steps into a real bath and is bathed in what appears to be soot or dyed sand by her female servant. Finis. Méliès' speciality was the trick film. He adapted some of his tricks from the magic theatre and from still photography, and invented others of his own. The use in the postcard of retouching, photomontage and collage is analogous to Méliès' camera magic. And like postcards, Méliès' films were often hand-tinted.

We have been talking about the general meaning of picture postcards in this introduction. In the next few chapters we try to strip particular meanings from our "feelthy peectures". Let the undressing commence . . .

1

I love you, he said

Somebody once said that the man who has never undressed a woman wearing turn-of-the-century clothes can know neither real love nor the joy of life. Jean Cocteau likened the aftermath of such a disrobing to the scene of a murder. And describing two formidable and famous beauties of the day in a restaurant he wrote: "Armour, escutcheons, carcans, corsets, whalebones, braids, épaulières, greaves, thighpieces, gauntlets, corselets, pearl baldricks, feather bucklers, satin, velvet and bejewelled halters, coats of mail–these knights-at-arms bristling with tulle, rays of light and eyelashes, these sacred scarabs armed with asparagus holders, these samurais of sable and ermine, these cuirassiers of pleasure who were harnessed and caparisoned early in the morning by robust soubrettes, seemed incapable, as they sat stiffly opposite their hosts, of extracting anything from an oyster beyond the pearl." Our postcards depict just such seductions, kisses, bathtime and bedtime.

An extraordinary thing about the cards is that it is difficult to understand what is really going on in many of them. Of course the "scenario" of our first set, numbered (1) to (5), is on the face of it extremely simple: a suitor watches a maid undress her mistress; the lady invites him in and they embrace. But what is *really* taking place? What does the maid's expression mean in (1)? And what is the suitor pointing at? Is the lady in (3) asking our approval before inviting the man in? The aesthetic conventions, even the concept of feminine beauty, are not ones we share today. The stylised gestures which sometimes lack significance, the strange setting and alien furnishings, the chasteness of it all, these things contribute to the ambiguity of the images. We are not watching just a seduction, we are watching something much more fantastic than that, a mime with a mystery to it.

Why are the players in this simple drama so like the dummies in some wax museum? The answer, probably, is that gestures are frozen because they had to be: in order that the photographer might get the picture he wanted an exposure of a second or so was needed, since he demanded sharp focus throughout (depth-of-field), and the only lighting he used was the sun shining through the studio skylight. It is this gentle light from above that gives the cards a particular beauty.

The setting in (1) seems to be a conventionalised one, if (6) is anything to go by. There are many common elements: the window through which the suitor watches, the occasional table with a vase of roses on it, the pile of underclothes tossed onto a chair, the suitor in dress clothes, the mistress wearing her chemise off the shoulder and a string of pearls.

The bourgeois milieu of (1) to (6) is substituted in (7) to (9) by a more proletarian one. Called "New Year's Day in a Garret" the card is postmarked 3.11.08, which means that it was not sent as a New Year greeting (postcards took the place of Christmas and birthday cards then). The implication is that this couple's New Year Resolution is to abstain from abstinence. Their surroundings are ruder than those in the last set, a chamber pot, stove, and crumpled mattress are conspicuous—this was, after all, the age of Zola—but their gestures seem less artificial than those of their "betters", they look *at* each other, not toward some imaginary horizon. And their lovemaking progresses farther in three cards than it does in five for the others. This set has a libertarian quality lacking in the last one. The lovers are equal partners in love. There is no suggestion of voyeurism, decorum, or sexual inequality.

The fact that (7) is franked does not necessarily mean that this frank card went through the post. In France, unlike England, it was possible to take a postcard to the post office, have it franked, then take it away to put in an album unposted. Some collectors, known as "philocartophiliacs", preferred to collect cards with post-marked stamps on the picture side.

Our next set, (10) to (14), has a similarly egalitarian spirit. A postman delivers a letter to a young lady who is dressing. She wags a finger at his advances. He pulls her onto his knee. She goes behind a screen—why we don't know!—to take off the rest of her clothes and put on some of his. By the end the young lady is almost naked and the postman is wearing her hat, feather boa and her knickers. Good humour and spirited playing characterise this set. The joke lies in the couple's cross dressing. Look where the postman's *képi* is in (14)! Seduction by a visiting trades-man, with its overtones of class-consciousness, was a popular post-card genre. The small strip of unoccupied space at the bottom of each image is where you wrote your message. These are "un-divided back" cards, and someone has written "1903" on them. In (15) another postman kisses another lady, probably in the same studio (the chair on which she kneels appears in the other set).

It wasn't always indoors that the indoor studio described. Outdoors came indoors in a set like "The Song of the Golden Corn", (16) to (21). The accompanying verses, however, do not always relate to the images:

1.–O fortunate young man who, under the burning summer skies, wanders through the beautiful Beauce countryside, only to surprise a pretty peasant girl of twenty!

2.–Ah! And in that solitude youth knows how to sing the sweet and poetic song of the golden corn!

3.–So as not to be seen the young people settle down in the shade of the tall sheaves, and each says in turn: "Is it really true that you love me?"

4.–Although troubled by such tender words the young girl is always heedful! . . . She is right, for as the young man strokes her gently she feels shivers of pleasure to hear him speak of love!

5.–When the time for parting comes, the young girl bursts into tears because she is thinking of her friend's possible faithlessness!

6.–The young man reassures her as best he can for so long that night surprises them in the field, and they fall asleep in each other's arms without noticing that the evening breeze is bending the golden corn and occasionally lifting the light material of the young girl's skirt!

The sunlight used to illuminate the decor gives it a naturalness that even the painted sky and crumpled canvas on the floor cannot completely dispel. After our eyes have taken in the real props they come up against the canvas "earth" and the painted backdrop, which severely limits the physical depth of the image, even though it alludes to a greater depth. Such differing kinds of illusion – which were, after all, common in postcards, in portrait photography, the theatre and the early cinema – manage to exist harmoniously and even give the images a special metaphysical quality. The commentary tells us about the evening breeze, but the corn does not move; we hear about nightfall, but the sunlight stays. Yet without the commentary what would we think was happening in (21)?

Possibly the most lugubrious set we have seen is the one of the seduction of a princess, (22) to (27). Here her frozen gestures are all too unambiguous: "alarm", "shame", "resignation". The only surprising thing about the set is the anachronistic decor (cf. the oil-lamp on the right) and the coy turning around of the chair in (27), with the attendant "ballet" of hands. The bed in the background is cleverly represented in foreshortening, though.

The same backdrop is used in another set, (28) to (33). And the chiropodist is played by the same actor as in (10). The same lace drape hangs in (10) too; and the chair on which the lady sits is sat upon in (22). Nevertheless, the "chiropodist" set is at least one year later. The cards are "divided backs", introduced in France in 1904, and the actor's hair has receded since his earlier appearance. The broad tone of this "cinematic" narrative was also found in the burlesque films about the picaresque adventures of "Boireau", "Rigadin", "Calino" and "Max" (played by Max Linder, who became a libidinous chiropodist in one of his movies), that were popular before the Great War.

Dating erotic postcards is often difficult, for the clues that ladies' costumes might give are rarely present since the clothes themselves, beyond the off-the-shoulder shift, are seldom worn for long. The hats that the otherwise typically dressed maidens wear in (34) and (35) date the postcards around 1909. Hats by this time were large and decorated with flowers and feathers. One society for the protection of wildlife proposed that instead of killing birds for their plumage carrots, artichokes, turnips and other vegetables would do just as well for ornamenting hats.

Our *ménage-à-trois* is set upon the top deck, or *impériale*, of an omnibus on the Madeleine to Bastille route. The omnibus was an obvious place for an erotic encounter because the stairway to the upper deck was open to all eyes, and it became a popular pastime for *les Messieurs de la plate-forme* to ogle the ascending lady passengers. In Berlin the police demanded that the stairway be masked from the public gaze, and one official proposed that ladies wishing to sit upstairs should wear divided skirts.

Are we meant to feel empathy with any of the characters? The man in the boater seems to be master of the situation and two women, yet something else is attracting his attention. The ladies oblige by removing their clothes, but they too seem to have other things on their mind. This lackadaisical, almost disinterested approach tends to dissipate the eroticism of the cards. We are left with little to appreciate but the symmetrical composition of (35).

After Baudelaire, and up to the time of André Breton, Paris served as the stamping-ground of the *flâneur*, the wanderer in search of the unexpected, the marvellous, the erotic. For the poet on foot the city became a paradise of chance encounters, strange events, mysterious sights. The *flâneur*, it has been said, went "botanising on the asphalt", and the Parisian *passages* were his happiest hunting-grounds.

A little tired after a morning spent in the pursuit of the unexpected our bowler-hatted pedestrian stops to rest for a moment on a convenient bench. Soon his attention is captured by the sight of a well-turned leg. The lady to whom it belongs has stopped to adjust her stocking. Perhaps she did not see our *flâneur* (who is hidden behind his newspaper). On the other hand, perhaps she did . . . Within five postcards the lady is barely clothed at all, and sitting on the knee of our hero, who has taken off his bowler.

The rapid courtship of the two lovers in (36) to (40) takes the form of some awkward posturing by both parties. Unhealthy exhibitionism and a desire to publicly defile women may appear to be the meaning of the cards, but we don't believe it is. These are simple wish-fulfillment scenes described in a naive language that is often clumsy; still, the images do possess an untainted eroticism and a simple, joyful spirit that no longer exists in our culture. The cards in this set are hand-tinted (see the colour plates), and the pretty girl looks as if she's wearing a strawberry on her head, her fashionable hat having been rather brashly coloured.

In all the "seduction" cards the participants act out their fantasies in the worlds that contain only themselves (and the person looking at the card). No other people intrude into these scenarios: the world exists solely for the lovers. How could a *lady* possibly undress in the street unless the street was empty? This absence of people, especially in the alfresco scenes where one might expect to see them, lends an enigmatic, surrealistic quality to things.

The younger Dumas coined the phrase *le demi-monde* to describe the "half-world" of the kept woman. Also known as *les cocottes* and, less charitably, as *les horizontales*, these beautiful and cultured courtesans dominated the world of fashion in *fin-de-siècle* Paris. "A cocotte," wrote Roger Shattuck, "had not arrived in her profession until she had inspired at least one suicide, unsuccessful of course, and three or four duels, and had *déniaisé* (initiated) her lover's eldest son."

The *demi-mondaine* was meticulous about her appearance. Her toilette was part of her mystique, and became part of the imagery associated with her. Painters like Degas and *La Vie Parisienne* illustrators like Gerbault explored this bathtime imagery. And it found its way quite naturally into the iconography of the French card.

In (41) to (46) a lady removes her stockings, tests the water, takes off her chemise and sits down in the bath. A real sponge is held in a real basket against a painted drape. She isn't near enough to reach it so the photographer and his assistant move bath and her nearer. The statutory pile of discarded clothes (underwear prominent) rests on a stool nearby. Just as our *cocotte* takes the sponge her beau enters, in top hat, frock coat and monocle. He has flowers to give her as well as his heart, he says. This latter-day Venus in the waves and white enamel has a bouquet of flowers, not the roses in the wind that Botticelli's shell-borne Venus gets.

The two cards with the gent on them, (45) and (46), have been stamped and franked (perhaps mailed, judging from the message on the front). They are dated 1908. The framing of (41) to (43) is erratic: the edge of the backcloth, complete with handle, can be seen at the left.

The same actress, carpet and cushion appear in what is the most vulgar of our cards (47). Here the lady has just filled her chamberpot and is putting it into a commode. There is bathos and humour in the presence of the white marble statue and the white porcelain potty.

It is a truism that the Great War marked the end of an era. The years immediately after 1914 represent the picture postcard's final fling. Erotic cards flourished openly alongside more jingoistic subjects, the aim of both being to support the flagging spirits of the fighting forces and the loved ones they had left behind. In a beautifully tinted card that reverses the normal order of things a soldier back from the front relaxes in the bath—we know he's a soldier because his helmet sits on the shelf above—and his lady friend, cigarette in hand, poses beside him. The caption reads:
To dream and to speak a thousand heartfelt words,

This moment of calm, the prelude to bliss.

Notwithstanding the *galante* gestures, there is a *real* quality about the bath itself, about the mirror and glass shelf, the plumbing, the tiles on the wall and the linoleum on the floor, that represents a complete break from the artifice and approximations of earlier studio shots. This greater realism, existing side by side with the usual repertoire of melodramatic poses, somehow captures the bathos and despair of the period.

A sketchily drawn card (see the colour plates) translates the simple wish fulfillments, born of separation, in a forthright way. It depicts "The Meal the *Poilu* Dreams About". (The *poilu* was the French equivalent of the "Tommy"). The menu consists of "a much desired *hors d'oeuvre*. A woman at last! Plump chicken! Fresh vegetables!! Wine!!!" The menu has a lot of *double entendre* on it too.

In all the cards discussed so far the photographer made sure of one thing: that when he pressed the shutter the whole of his subject was represented. We never see anything but the complete woman or the complete man. The portrait of the pretty girl (48) is an instance of this aesthetic rule. There she is, slap bang in the middle of the picture.

Bearing this cliché in mind, a card like (49) absolutely leaps up off the page at us. It shows a girl's stockinged leg resting over the arm of a chair. The image has the same sort of impact that the first close-ups had for cinema audiences, who are said to have physically recoiled from the sight of such enormously enlarged features. The card is probably late (c. 1920?). In it the photographer has taken his camera to that which interests him most. He has described his fetish.

Discoursing on the medical implications of fetishism Havelock Ellis proposed that the "imaginative lover" conceived of an erotic symbol (a stocking and shoe, say) as something that was part of the object of his desire. That is to say, *because* the loved one was actually wearing them when lovemaking began the stocking and shoe became eroticised. For the "unsound" personality, though, the symbol became detached from the loved one who is no longer desired at all, and came to signify desire itself. The stocking and shoe became objects of desire in their own right. "When," says Ellis in his sober jargon, "the woman is ignored and the mere symbol is an adequate and even preferred stimulus to detumescence the pathological condition becomes complete."

Now, we are not making a medical judgment about the photographer who took (49), or the kind of man who would buy it—anyway, we happen to find it one of the most erotic cards in the book—but it is interesting that Ellis spotted a distinction like that, between the whole (and the wholesome) and the part. The startling quality of (49) is due to more than its aesthetic novelty: after all the model's left leg in (48) rests over the edge of the chair in much the same way except that it is attached to her body, and does not appeal in itself to any fetishistic feelings we might have.

"It would be best to be like these two," some unknown person has written on the picture of a man in braces planting a kiss on the shoulder of a pretty girl (50). That writer was probably a soldier, for this genre, "The Kiss" (*le baiser*), was popular during the Great War. It communicated a simple message, "I love you", in a sentimental way. The couple, naked from the armpits up, are generally seen suspended in an idealised bit of sky called Heaven, their disembodies entwined in a kiss. The romantic effect was achieved by airbrushing, and the ethereal space surrounding the lovers was used as a dark setting for some light verses:

Tell me! Oh, tell me that you love me!
My heart, that nothing more can fright,
Will ever know to love you dearly.
You, whose kiss planted on my mouth
Has caused me to be born again . . . and then to die! (51)

Or,

This divine *cri de coeur*, to relish the kiss,
Is to drink at the cup, to be enchanted by bliss. (52)

And,

Eyes looking into eyes, my lips holding sway,
Our hearts in ecstasy, we banish our cares away. (53)

Did René Magritte know cards like these when he came to paint "The Lovers" in 1928? Magritte's surrealistic oil represents a girl sitting in a landscape. Her lips are pressed against the lips of her lover, but his head is all there is of him, his body is invisible.

We close this chapter with a well-acted and elegantly produced bedroom set, (54) to (57).

"Your lovely clear eyes will serve me as stars," says the pyjama-ed husband, and blows out a distinctly phallic candle (the room stays light). His wife reclines on her pillow, looking bored.

"It is not the hour yet for closing the eyes," he leers. She, shifting her weight to the other elbow, is not so sure.

The next card is set many sleepless hours later, for the now desperate husband is saying, "The sun invites us to sing the song of kisses!" Missus sinks into the pillow.

"Why refuse me the ultimate caress?" the desperate spouse hisses, and ruefully snatches at her nightdress, exposing shoulder and breast.

"Because I feel like it!" is written all over her face . . .

The beauty of this set is that the refined performances of both players clashes with the written dialogue and serves to parody its lush language, which is typical of the period and of many of the postcards we have already looked at. The serialised visuals complete with dialogue recall the comic strips, and anticipate the kind known as *fumetti* which use photographic, rather than drawn, images.

Other almost identical examples of this genre do not take themselves so lightly, although the caption to (58) has paradox on its side: "Happiness," it reads, "needs no caption".

22

5

6

4

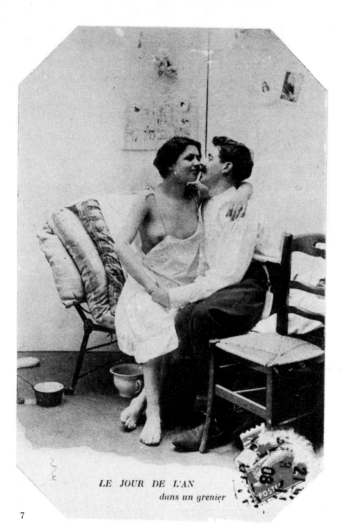

LE JOUR DE L'AN
dans un grenier

7

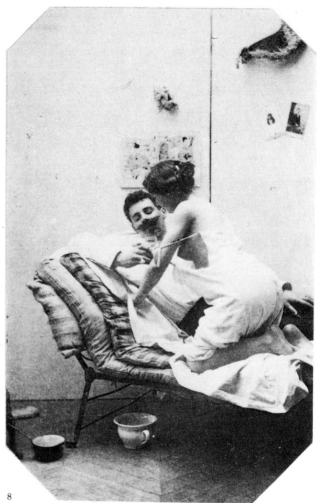

8

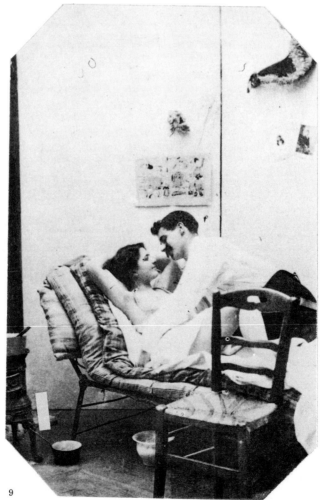

9

10

1903

1903

11

1903

13

1903

12

26

14

1903

15

LA CHANSON DES BLÉS D'OR

1 – Heureux jeune homme, qui, sous le brûlant soleil d'été, traverse les belles campagnes de la Beauce, et fait peur à une jolie paysanne de vingt ans!

16

2 – Ah! par cette solitude, que la jeunesse la sait bien chanter la douce et poëtique chanson des blés d'or!

17

28

3 - *Pour ne pas être aperçu de loin, les deux jeunes gens, s'installent à l'ombre des hautes gerbes - et chacun dit à son tour: «est-ce bien vrai que vous m'aimez!»*

18

4 - *La jeune fille, quoique troublée par de si tendres aveux, est toujours attentive!... elle a raison, car le jeune homme est si caressant, qu'elle ressent un frisson de plaisir à l'entendre parler d'amour!*

19

5 - *Au moment de se séparer la jeune fille fondit en larmes, en pensant à l'inconstance possible de son ami!*

20

6 - *Le jeune homme la rassura de son mieux et si longuement que la nuit les surprit dans les champs et qu'il s'endormirent dans les bras de l'un de l'autre, sans s'apercevoir que la brise du soir inclinait les blés d'or et soulevait parfois la frêle jupe de toile de la jeune fille!*

21

22

23

24

25

26

27

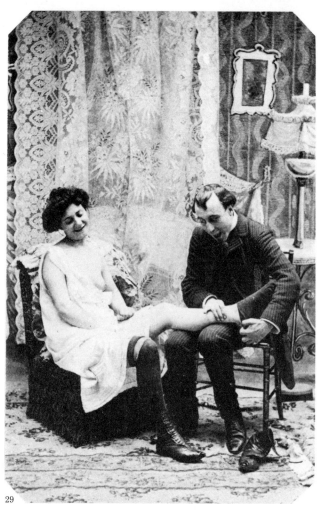

29

28

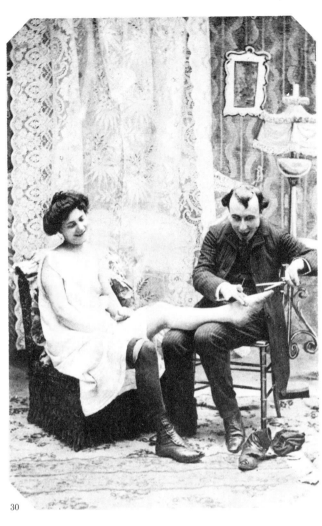

30

31

33

32

34

35

36

37

38

39

40

41

42

43

44

45

46

47

48

49

Dis-moi! oh! dis-moi que tu m'aimes!
Mon cœur, que plus rien n'effarouche,
A jamais saura te chérir,
Toi, dont le baiser sur ma bouche,
M'a fait renaître... et puis mourir!

DIX
446

51

Baiser d'Amour

54/5

NÉO-PHOT
PARIS

50

Le Baiser

Savourer le baiser, ce divin cri du cœur.
C'est boire à la coupe enchantée du bonheur.

52   113

Le Baiser

Les yeux dans les yeux, mes lèvres pressant les tiennes
De nos cœurs en extase, banissons nos peines

53   265\2

Tes yeux pleins de clarté me serviront d'étoiles ?...

54

L'heure n'est pas venue où l'on ferme les yeux !...

55

Le soleil nous invite aux chansons des baisers !...

56

57

58

2

I serve you, she said

The pictures of the slave markets of Ancient Rome and of the Orient that go to make up this chapter project a watered-down version of the passionate Romanticism of 19th century France, the period of Delacroix, Gautier, Borel and Flaubert: "O Nero, your gilded villa is only a filthy stable beside the palace I have built. My wardrobe is fitted out in greater style than yours, Heliogabalus. My circuses are noisier and bloodier than yours; my perfumes more acrid and penetrating; my slaves more powerful and numerous. I have harnessed naked courtesans to my chariot. I have walked over the bodies of men with a step as light as your own."

By the end of the century the images conjured up by Théophile Gautier's purple prose (from *Mademoiselle de Maupin*), tired from a trip through the dusty salons of academic painting, had found their way into the postcard. The sensual language of the Romantics showed them to be the heirs of the Marquis de Sade. Refined vices and atrocious crimes were part of the Romantics' conception of their spiritual and very distant homelands. By the time the postcard artisans got hold of the idea this imaginative dimension had long since disappeared and a more exploitable eroticism had taken its place.

A fiddle (actually it's a lyre) figures so prominently in our first set of cards, (59) to (64), that no one could fail to spot the reference. Our Nero reclines, like all Romans do, on a bed of animal skins (connotations of bestiality) and other stuffs. A trader offers him two slaves. The girls, who don't know whether to laugh or cry, are bought by the Emperor, who tickles the glum one under the chin. The really remarkable thing about the girls is their posture—the result, no doubt, of the corsets they wore when not posing for naughty postcards. The whole set is beautifully tinted by hand using stencils, a technique also common in films of the period (see *Plain or coloured, Sir?*).

For all its banality this set has something honourable about it: it makes no attempt to disguise the fact that it is exploiting a sexual fantasy; the girls are seen to be nothing more nor less than enslaved objects. On the other hand, the academic painters whose works served as visual sources for postcards like these never admitted the eroticism they exploited, but tried to disguise it. The delirious eroticism of these supposedly "chaste", "heroic", "noble" compositions is only today being recognised.

Some salon painters specialised in Oriental subjects. Their work was part of a contemporary preference for things exotic. France's colonial expansion in North Africa was taking place at this time. Travellers were returning from strange lands with photographs and, later, movies. At the 1889 Exposition a Cairo street was reconstructed in Paris and Egyptians were imported to live in it and perform the belly dance! For the common man the Orient conjured up at least one idea: the image of the potent potentate, the man who owned and "fulfilled" not one but many women.

A pasha's harem is the setting of our next set, (65) to (70). (A pasha was a high-ranking Turk, a military commander or the governor of a province.) A janissary stands guard at the entrance to the harem. Two of the inmates show themselves (65). In (66) we meet the pasha. His domain is suggested by Persian carpets, a hookah, and a handprint (!) on the wall (67). Although the girls grin and bare it they don't really like the man: indeed, one of them appears to be pouring tea on him in (67). Their hearts belong to "the gallant janissary" (68). Unfortunately our set is incomplete from now on. We leap from tableau IV to tableau VII and then to tableau IX. The narrative goes haywire. By (69) one of the concubines has done something wrong, for her hands are bound and her arm is held in the grip of an attendant eunuch. The pasha is meting out justice. In (70) things have gone from bad to worse. Someone is getting "unexpected help" from the gallant janissary, but who? the pasha, the guilty concubine (who is playing dead), or the eunuch? The last image in the series looks like a detail from Rochegrosse's "Last Days of Babylon", the main attraction at the 1891 Paris Salon, which was indebted in turn to Delacroix's "Sardanapalus". The vast and seething tableaux of both enormous paintings have here been rendered down into a $5\frac{1}{2}$ by $3\frac{1}{2}$ inch photograph.

Nine was probably the number of cards in the complete "pasha" set, for what looks like a complete set of nine cards depicting a slave market scene forms our next group, (71) to (79). It appears to be the product of the same studio—the decorated drape in the background is in (65) too—but is later in date and more refined in production values. We, as spectator-voyeurs, have been put amongst the bidders at the market. We sit in the second row behind four Orientals. First one girl, then another, is brought on and her charms exhibited. We watch as the bidders bid. One of them has a magnifying glass to better examine the merchandise (76). Gold changes hands (77). A disgruntled customer takes one last feel of the goods he nearly bought (78) and for this he is set upon (79). The repetitious narrative is sustained by the comic gusto of all concerned, but what a commonplace fantasy! Not cynical, just banal and unimaginative. Everything in the picture is tinted, even the enigmatic object that looks like a gramophone horn (see the colour plates).

One man to one woman was the equation usually made in the *I love you, he said* chapter. Not one woman, but women are usually the thing in this chapter. Men are out-numbered or absent, but always in control whether it be in physical form playing slave-traders or tyrants, or behind the scenes as the orchestrators of coarse imaginings about male potency and dominance.

The combatants in "The Circus Games" are women, not men, and initially have all the personality of the symbols on the "tails" of coins. The eroticism of this set, (80) to (84), lies in the Amazonian role the women play; in the contrast between helmets, shields, weapons and female flesh, and the contrast between the fierce and dangerous nature of the contest and the usual role of women. Eloquently and personably played throughout in a simple but effective setting, the last image of the victor and the vanquished has a perversity that is special. The naked Amazon seems to be asking us to give the thumbs-up or thumbs-down. She is ready to execute the defeated warrior if we say so. This scenario still cuts ice today. A movie called *The Arena*, directed by Steve Carver in 1973, exploits just this kind of eroticism.

There is a Sapphic element in "The Circus Games" which must have tickled the imaginations of the people who looked at the cards then. The idea of lesbianism was, and is, a common fantasy for both men and women. Guy de Maupassant, the late 19th century writer, painted a pretty picture of the contemporary taste for things Sapphic in his story "Paul's Mistress": "A canoe covered with an awning and manned by four women came slowly down the current. She who rowed was petite, thin, faded, in a cabin boy's costume, her hair drawn up under an oilskin hat. Opposite her a lusty blonde, dressed as a man, with a white flannel jacket, lay upon her back at the bottom of the boat, her legs in the air, resting on the seat at each side of the rower. She smoked a cigarette, while at each stroke of the oars, her chest and her stomach quivered, shaken by the stroke. At the back, under the awning, two handsome girls, tall and slender, one dark and the other fair, held each other by the waist as they watched their companions.

"A cry arose from La Grenouillère, 'There's Lesbos,' and all at once a furious clamour, a terrifying scramble took place; the glasses were knocked down; people clambered onto the tables; all in a frenzy of noise bawled: 'Lesbos! Lesbos! Lesbos!' " Unfortunately Paul is not like everybody else. He is so mortified to find that his mistress has a lady for a lover that he drowns himself!

There is a suggestion of Sapphism in the next set of cards, which show a maid and her mistress in search of an errant insect,

(85) to (89). This tale was popular in the cinema too: Charles Pathé made a film of it called *The Flea*, which lasted for one minute and featured the actress Willy of the Olympia Theatre, Paris.

"Quick! Undress me," exclaims the lady with a smile on her face, "I can feel something biting me." The maid removes the mistress' bodice. "Oh, madame, there it is! But wait, I think it's jumped onto me now!" The mistress removes the maid's bodice, and takes up the search. "Oh, the villain!" says the maid, pointing, "it's just jumped into your stocking." Surrounded now by discarded clothing, the lady eventually tracks down the insect: "Ah, got it at last!" Smiles are just about all the women are wearing.

Sexual goings-on between masters and servants were a common subject in erotic literature and art then. The really amusing thing today about this aristocratic striptease is that a flea should be the pretext for it.

There is more than a suggestion of Sapphism in (90) to (95). These blatant cards provided two females for the price of one, with a bogus fantasy thrown in for good measure.

The chains of the women "serving" us in the next few cards are real ones. But they are mythic ones too which bind our Three Graces too decoratively to be uncomfortable. The photographer who took the three pictures, (96) to (98), undermined the mythological dimension of his subject matter by posing the models in an obviously erotic way. These are real young girls offering themselves to us in symmetrical poses and gazes that seem innocent enough now but must have been powerful then.

G. Mouton's drawing, "Parat's Private Property" (99), depicts a lady bound hand and foot by chains set into the wall of a small, bare cell. The verse reads:

Afraid of being cuckolded Parat the chemist
Places a great big padlock on his wife's virtue.

Fierce spikes to discourage wandering palms stick from the wife's scant clothing. She wears a chastity belt and a tight collar. The theme of bondage illuminates this light-hearted perversity. The lady does not seem too unhappy to submit to her tying-up. Her masochism, her delight in being beaten, is implied by the whip hanging on the wall.

Women chained, women sold into slavery, images like these refer obliquely to the suffragettes who were chaining themselves to railings at the same time as cards like these were circulating. Although the remoteness in time and space of much of this imagery was used as a pretext for exposing the naked female body, that same imagery has in it the seeds of solidarity with the more concrete historical events referred to above.

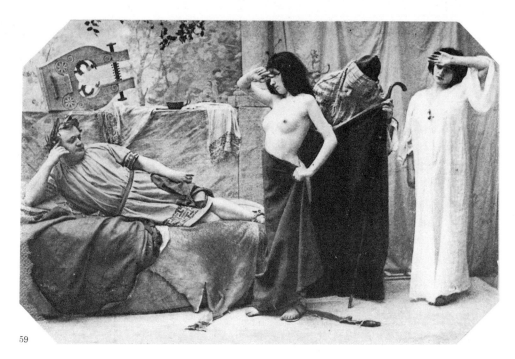

59

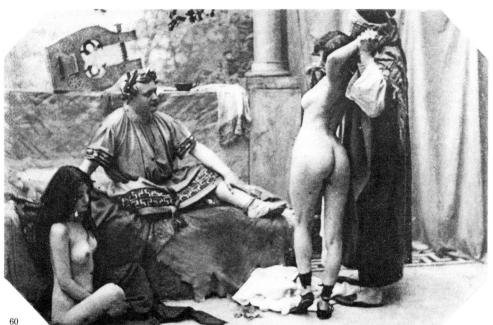

60

61

62

63

64

Entrée du harem

65

Le Pacha

66

54

Scène d'intérieur

67

Le galant Janissaire

68

55

La Justice du Pacha

69

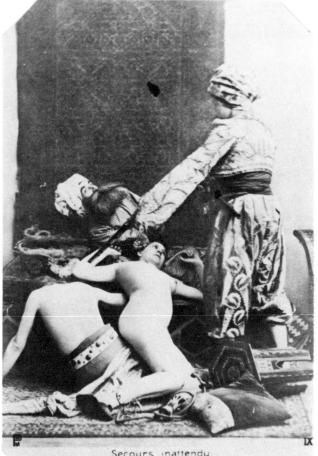

Secours inattendu

70

56

71

72

74

73

75

76

78

77

60

79

80

81

82

62

83

84

I. Vite déshabillez-moi, je sens quelque chose
qui me pique.

85

II. Oh! Madame, je l'aperçois.

86

64

III. Regardez, Madame, il me semble
qu'elle vient de sauter sur moi.

87

IV. Oh! la vilaine! elle vient de se faufiler
dans votre bas.

88

V. Ah! enfin je la tiens!

89

65

90

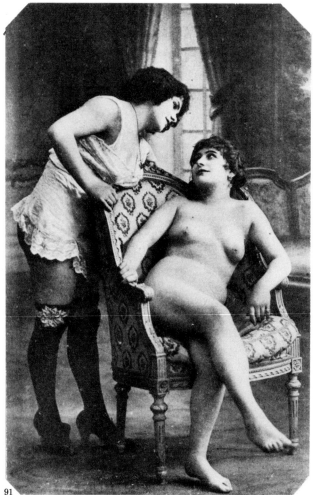

91

92

66

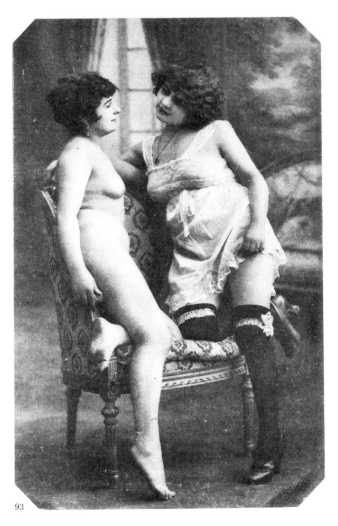

93

94

95

67

96

97

98

G. Mouton

La Sequestrée de Parat ?

Dans la crainte du cocufiage, le pharmacien Parat ;
Sur la vertu de sa femme y place un gros cadenas '

99

3

I worship you, he said

Chains, real or imagined, by no means monopolise the postcard image of women. This image could give way to a gentler, idealised view that is completely captivating. The polarity of the two ideas mirrored the opposing conceptions of art then current. On the one hand there was Naturalism, "with its odour of the kitchen and of misery". On the other was Symbolism, "with its ring-laden fingers" (Waldberg). The poet Paul Eluard—who, with fellow sur-realists Breton and Brunius had a large collection of post-cards—has given us an inventory of the shapes our idealised woman might take: "Child-women, *femmes-fleurs*, star-women, women of flame, flotsam, huge billows of love and of the dream, the flesh of poets, solar statues, masks of night, white rose-bushes in the snow, servants, governesses, chimerae, radiant virgins, perfect courtesans, legendary princesses, passers-by, they are man's strength and his *raison d'être*; they beatify his feebleness, bring joy, make cares disappear."

The distinction between the naturalism of the cards already discussed and the (organic) symbolism of the cards we are about to look at extends to the question of technique. Photography is the obvious way to communicate naturalism. More graphic means were used to give form to our idealised woman. The imagination requires the intervention of the human hand to make its workings actual. Our first three cards are proof of this.

The first, "The Butterfly", represents a naked woman, with antennae and wings, holding a flower (100), and was made in the following way: a model was posed in front of a painted backdrop of a landscape; the cameraman focused on the girl, leaving the

70

background out of focus, and clicked the shutter; a vignetted print was made, which entailed shading off the image around the edges; a draughtsman drew on the butterfly wings and antennae in monochrome inks, and did the lettering in white; a retoucher stippled out the model's pubic hair; finally, the finished picture was rephotographed and sepia prints made. The example we have has been stencil tinted by hand (see the colour plates). Although we will never know how much of it was his, M. Boulanger was proud enough of the postcard to sign it.

In "The Carnation" (101) a naked model has been welded at the middle to the centre of a blooming carnation. Superimposition, photomontage and airbrushing make this strange graft possible. Perhaps M. Boulanger autographed his cards by hand because his third, "The Ant" (102), bears a signature that is different to the other two, which are different to each other. Our winged ant, who can play the lute, sits on a treetrunk beside a lake. She seems to have come into the world in much the same way as her butterfly sister.

Women as butterflies, ants and blossom: natural images like these suggest the idea of a fragile and short-lived beauty. The fact that flowers and insects are partners in germination adds a wholly erotic ambiance to these more than human forms. The spirit of Georges Méliès permeates these postcards too. The butterfly-women in his films came from the conjuring theatre, where such analogies were common.

The decor of the next two cards, (103) and (104), could have come straight from a Méliès movie. The same vigorous brushwork and tranquil imagery is here. Called "The Spider", these two cards are probably part of a larger set, for the precise meaning of the images escapes us. In (103) a beautiful naked girl lies by a lake and watches a spider sitting at the centre of his web. By (104) the spider has spun a larger web and the water plants have grown. The spider, too, is edging towards the girl, who stretches out her arms in horror or expectation. Because some female spiders eat the males after mating the spider as a symbol usually signifies the *femme-fatale*. But this postcard spider has, we imagine, a male identity. What the spider means then, and what the girl's response is, we do not know.

The Arcadian tone of women symbolised as flora and fauna sometimes degenerated into a more sentimentalised, censorial idealisation. In (105) to (109) a lady holds a variety of garlands and a snake, and the same "artistic" pose. The hand of the retoucher has left its mark here. The model, posed in front of a black background, holds a hoop above and behind her head. This halo was later garnished by the retoucher who painted roses, pansies and daisies on it. We know she isn't wearing a *maillot* because we can see her toes, but the general effect is the same, for the retoucher has removed all the offending features from her body and nipped in her waist. Imagine being born like that! A serpent is one of the things our Eve holds. And in a similar example (110), published by the famous Reutlinger company, a long-haired goddess grips a mirror which transmits light.

There really is a tremendous difference between the floral and faunal women and these sentimentalised deities. In (101), "The Carnation", for instance, the woman was actually part of the flower – she symbolised the profound union of Woman and Nature – and the idea of fertility was evoked by this analogy. On the visual level we saw the techniques that were to hand being used in an imaginative way to make a meaningful idea pictorial. On the other hand the flowers on the garland held by one of our bowdlerised beauties have a merely decorative, vacuous appeal. A sense of shame, of a repressed mentality, characterises (106), which has all the subtlety and eloquence of religious kitsch. The same pictorial means have been used to censor, not liberate, the imagination.

Other examples of a purely decorative eroticism are given by three cards from an incomplete set, (111) to (113). The poses of the three nymphs with their flying drapes probably refer to some academic painting or other. The unusual layout of the cards suggests that these are "undivided backs": you wrote in the unoccupied space to the right of the ladies. The organic arabesques underline the equation between women and plant forms that was in the air at the time. The English call this "Art Nouveau"; the French call it "Modern 'Style".

Another card (114) from the same studio (S.I.P., Paris) and period (pre-1904) is signed by the photographer, J. Orieky, and the man who drew the pretty surround, Paul de Lys. The artist has planted the border with lilies. (Archaic French for lily is *"lys".*) This flower, with its phallic stamen, is a symbol of purity, of virginity. Our postcard, which goes deeper into symbolic connotation than its near neighbours, conjures up the symbolist poet Viélé-Griffin's lines:

I have decorated my kingdom with lilies
As frail as virgins or as joys.

The veil is an ideal erotic accessory, because it conceals and accentuates at the same time. The disturbing thing about (115) and (116) is that the veil, another symbol of virginity, is pulled back to reveal the face of a woman no longer young.

Although superficially similar, there is a world of difference between the garlanded deities and the goddesses of our next set. In the first card, "The Comet" (117), a goddess protects her face from a speeding comet. In the second, "The Pole Star" (118), a divinity standing on Saturn points to the Pole Star. In the third, "The Milky Way" (119), a goddess sits on a galactic magic carpet. Like the earlier group these goddesses are posed against an ostensibly black background, but unlike them our goddesses are also women, they are animated, tangible, natural. The artist has used his skill to send a woman up into the heavens. There is an impossible and purely poetic jump in scale from the infinity of space to an even bigger divinity. This spatial relation is as marvellous as the mythology that inspires it.

"A mask," said Oscar Wilde, "is always more expressive than a face." Perhaps this accounts for the truly bizarre quality of the set we print called "I Want to Hug the Moon!", (120) to (122), which could perhaps be the title of a since forgotten song. Like the last set this has something to do with unexpected leaps in scale, in this case from the enormous saucer-like face of the Man in the Moon to the comic mask which is in turn out of proportion with the person who is wearing it. What is even more curious is that this is a woman. There is a further shift from the fixed smile and stare on the moon's face to the rigid cry and unblinking sorrow on the face of the mask to the expressive gestures of the bare-breasted girl, whose face we never see; and from the two-dimensional painted moon to the three-dimensional, hollow, *papier-mâché* mask to more solid, real flesh. This badly-proportioned creature is an androgyne. There is something genuinely shocking about a gargantuan male head and naked, little, female breasts being in such close and intimate proximity.

Our postcard images have such vitality, even perversity, that they stimulate the imagination to make equations that are always surreal. We find our gaze moving from one spot to another: from the cry frozen on the mask's lips to the peephole in the girl's clothing that reveals her breasts, for instance. Our ludicrous but moving androgyne stands before a roughly painted panorama of Paris: the Panthéon and Notre-Dame are prominent, but the Eiffel Tower is hidden until the last card between the lady's legs. We are certain that this erotic pun is an accidental one, although the clumsy scene-painter has made the Eiffel Tower more phallic, less insubstantial, than it really is . . .

For some strange reason we have put a man in the satellite which for countless mythological years has had feminine connotations. This "confusion" is repeated in the case of our moon's would-be lover, who has a male head on female shoulders. The meaning of it all is beyond solution, because it is so completely allusive and so genuinely enigmatic. But why try to solve it? We should be grateful for poetry, not try to explain it away.

Coming back to earth, "*Die Jungfrau*" is a fanciful portrait of the Swiss Alp (123). The peak, whose name in English means "The Virgin", is represented as just that, the rock metamorphosing into the reclining body of a fleshy maiden. A party of climbers is clambering all over her. They are pioneers who have violated her virgin state, for the woman-mountain covers her eyes with her hand in shame. This is a visual pun, giving pictorial form to the analogies frequently made between the landscape and the human body. We speak of the brow of the hill, the neck of the woods or, more pertinently, of mountainous breasts. The postcard artist extends these analogies to a whole and wholesome female figure. An amusing detail is meant to be the man standing on the Jungfrau's breasts. This is a German card, which proves that the French did not have a monopoly where eroticism was concerned. Scandinavia, too, had a finger in the naughty postcard pie.

A poor man's Alphonse Mucha drew our next card (124). It represents a woman exhaling a gas that swirls around her head like hair. Mucha often portrayed a similar beauty in his graphic work advertising "Job" cigarette papers. We prefer to think that our maiden is a zephyr, that oxygen is the substance she exhales. The visual pun between air and hair permits an erotic equation of fetishistic and elemental sexuality to be made.

In some cases graphic techniques were not necessary to paint a picture of idealised womanhood, the photographic means typical of our more naturalistic themes could do just as well. A photographed narrative, (125) to (130), tells the story of the sculptor Pygmalion who made a woman in marble and then fell in love with her. In (125) he prays to Venus for a bride who will look like the marble figure. The goddess answers his prayers, for in (127) Galatea comes to life and touches the sculptor's head. He ponders the problem in (128), and takes up his hammer and chisel to strike a last despairing blow (129) when suddenly his idealised woman bends down to embrace him. This crude retelling of the myth of Pygmalion escapes total condemnation to the dustbins of kitsch if we remember that the Ancient Greeks and Romans probably looked more like the postcard player (notwithstanding his moustache) than like the solid, grey, idealised sculptures that are left to us and which were in any case originally painted in flesh tints and wore coloured clothing. The Pygmalion myth refers to a certain moment in the development of Greek art, when a greater naturalism and individualism emerged. Sculpture appeared to be so lifelike as to actually possess life.

The trusty Havelock Ellis thought that falling in love with statues, or "Pygmalionism", was a "rare form of erotomania founded on the sense of vision and closely related to the allurement of beauty." Certainly the tone of our postcard set is as "chaste" as the contemporary academic art from which it sprang, and which itself sought justification in the distant and misunderstood ideals of Greco-Roman culture. Salon painters like Hoffman and Dantan portray Pygmalion sculptors at work. Woman is idealised in a sentimentalised way far removed from the earthy symbolism of many of our earlier examples, which refer to folk mythology rather than an ill-informed counterfeit art history.

To tell his story the set designer has used atmospheric objects like an oil-lamp, a lyre, and a pitcher, but try as he may the story looks as if it is set firmly in the life-class of a Parisian art school, c. 1905, not in Athens, c. 400 B.C.

"I worship you," *she* said: there are hints of Sapphism in the way the maid in "To Be Loved" idolises her mistress, (131) to (135). The running commentary goes like this:

I.–In the cool boudoir's bosom, at first light,
On a morn auspiciously pale,
Like a young fairy or flower white,
A child beauty smiles on the day.
II.–She is dressing. A graceful shudder
Courses through her like the shiver of a dream.
Against the sponge her young breast presses
While water runs down in a stream.
III.–Like a bride on the day of her wedding,
A mist of iris around her she'll assume,

While the sweet scent of rice powder
Coats dainty fingers with its perfume.
IV.–So sweet the hope one has at twenty!
This child wants to be beautiful, loved.
With her maid beside her this morning
Dreaming, by such grace extremely moved.
V.–A comb runs through her golden tresses,
Now she's all but finished dressing.
The mirror she holds reflects in her eyes
Happiness without end, infinite promise.

What infinite sadness, too, in the inequality between the two girls, which is registered so wilfully by the suitably plain servant! The first time we really meet the gaze of the young mistress is in the last card (135), when we see that she is looking at us in the mirror she holds. This heroine is like one of the somnambulistic women in a painting by Paul Delvaux. Indeed the not always bland verses emphasise the dreaminess of the early morning reverie, which is meant to be seen through a pallid erotic mist of rice powder and white lace.

A growing sophistication in decor and props, and an increasing eye for detail characterises the development of the photographic postcard. In the early days, c. 1900, canvas sheets covered the studio floor, backcloths were roughly painted, and furnishings meagre. In our next set, (136) to (140), the textural variety and detail of the images adds much to their appeal. The well-painted backdrop represents a woodland glade and a lake; a pile of stones stands on the left: they appear to consist of boxes covered by bark. The left edge of the outcrop can be seen in (136) and (139), a further instance of the careless framing that plagued many post-card productions. Turf planted with one or two bits of greenery has been laid on the studio floor.

The narrative depicts the undressing of a lady with a parasol. She is, presumably, about to take a dip in the painted lake behind her. Always on the lookout for peeping Toms, the woman lets her hair down in (139). She seems to be unaware that we are watching her, but in the last card she admits she knew all along when she returns our gaze. The metaphorical relation between Woman and Nature is made in a non-metaphorical, literal way.

We have already said that an erotic context can give a sexual charge to things that are commonplace and "neutral". We used the next set as an example of this process of "infection". It shows a naked girl at a window, (141) to (145). The series is permeated by a delightful naivety. We see the girl on the other side of a rickety window frame (141). She is outside, we take it, because the backcloth behind her represents a wooded landscape. But we think we are outside too, because on our side of the wall there is a carpenter's horse with plant pots and a watering can on it, and the window is bordered by climbing plants. In (142) the girl opens the window and, shading her eyes against the very gentle sunlight, looks towards the horizon, before showing off her charms (143). The climax of the series comes when she waters the flowers. This innocent, even clumsy, set has a radiant air to it.

LE PAPILLON

100

LA FOURMI

102

L'ŒILLET

101

103

104

105

106

107

78

108

109

110

79

111

112

113

114

115

116

82

117

118

119

J'veux embrasser la lune !

120

J'veux embrasser la lune !

121

J'veux embrasser la lune !

122

84

123

124

125

126

128

127

129

130

POUR ÊTRE AIMÉE

I. — Au sein du frais boudoir, en la clarté première
D'un demi-jour propice à sa fraîche pâleur,
Comme une jeune fée ou quelque blanche fleur,
Une beauté d'enfant sourit dans la lumière :

131

POUR ÊTRE AIMÉE

II. — Elle fait sa toilette. Un frisson gracieux
Palpite en elle ainsi que le frisson d'un songe,
Lorsque son jeune sein se cambre sous l'éponge,
Tandis que l'eau ruisselle en flots capricieux.

132

89

POUR ÊTRE AIMÉE

III. — Ainsi qu'une épousée au seuil du mariage,
Elle veut qu'autour d'elle un nuage d'iris
S'exhale, et le parfum de la poudre de riz
Imprègne ses doigts fins d'une senteur suave.

133

POUR ÊTRE AIMÉE

IV. — Il est si doux l'espoir que l'on porte à vingt ans,
L'enfant veut être belle en se sachant aimée,
Et sa femme de chambre est là, de temps en temps,
Rêveuse, et de sa grâce, elle même charmée.

134

90

POUR ÊTRE AIMÉE

V. — De ses cheveux, le peigne ondule l'or soyeux !
A présent la toilette est à moitié finie,
Le miroir qu'elle tient reflète avec ses yeux
D'un bonheur inéclos, la promesse infinie.

135

136

137

138

139

140

141

142

144

143

145

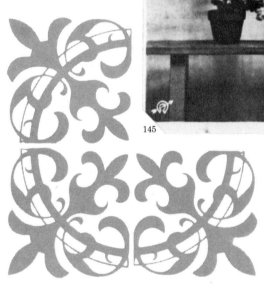

4

This means that, they say

Visual puns, double meanings, *double entendres*, "phallic symbols" and metaphors abound in the picture postcard. Dual meaning is a common feature of popular art and its great ally, caricature. The graphic freedom granted the popular artist enables him to stretch the bounds of possibility, to remake reality and its image in whatever capricious and poetic form he cares to choose. Analogy and eroticism are means to this end. Puns and double meanings propose that there is a kind of visual order based on the formal similarity of things. They encourage the imagination to make analogies between things that are perhaps not related at all.

"A Choice of Eggs" (146) suggests the visual similarity between a woman's breasts and two large eggs: "Please yourself. I'll let you choose which ones you want in your own time", says the verse. This is a special kind of pun where you see both of the objects in the punning equation side by side for comparison. This particular pun is based on the slight similarity between white oval breasts and white oval eggs, and the fact that both eggs and breasts are paired, or can be. The joke is that it's obvious which "eggs" we would choose. Visually, the postcard is unusual in that we don't see the girl from head to toe.

The genre of comparing female breasts to other things is an extensive one. In a pair of cards in our colour section an analogy between breasts and apples is hinted at. The cards are a modern dress version of the Garden of Eden myth. In a turfed studio with a wooded backcloth Eve, in stockings, pointed shoes and chemise stands on a ladder propped against a real tree trunk. From the branches hang apples. Eve is helped in her apple-picking by a suited Adam. In one of the cards he is being treated to the bite of an apple. His hand touches Eve's bare breast. The largely oral equation is made. In the other card Adam holds a tray which Eve is about to fill with apples or breasts. This card has all the ingredients of a well-known visual pun which consists of a lady holding a tray with apples and her breasts placed on it. The two things intermingle, and the suggestion is that they are the same. This image is iconographically related to Renaissance paintings by artists like Lorenzo Lippi and Bernardino Luino of Saint Agatha, the martyred saint whose breasts were cut from her body. She is usually portrayed bearing the severed breasts on a tray.

The exact meaning of (147) is not clear. The tambourine the model proffers is rather like a tray and brings to mind the kind of pun discussed above. A retoucher has pared the lady's figure down to its rather adolescent proportions. Her boyish face (recalling Sarah Bernhardt or a young Katherine Hepburn) adds to the allusiveness of the image.

Every schoolboy has heard of "phallic symbols". For psychoanalysts any long, erect thing can have a symbolic connotation as a phallus; anything resembling a vessel or box connotes a vagina. In the postcard phallic, or genital, symbolism can be either unconscious or blatant, manifest or latent.

Even an audience not brought up on the clichés of psychoanalysis would have seen the symbolism in (148). The joke must have been as apparent in 1905 as it is in 1975. Called "The Greasy Pole" the postcard depicts a naked woman shinning up a "long, erect thing". She is trying to get to the prizes hung above her:

If my hand can reach
The sack of gold
In this one last go,
I won't complain.

Perhaps the lady is clinging to a long-standing fallacy... The "sack of gold" is doubtless meant to be read as a *double entendre*.

The postcard artist did not invent all the puns and *double entendres* he used, many of them existed already. Nevertheless, he brought them even further into the public domain. The artist Fox drew a long series of cards called *Parisian Curiosities* that are notable for their amiable vulgarity and for the skilful way in which they are made.

Number 9 in the series depicted Sacré Coeur (149). Fox drew the back view of a lady sitting astride a circular frame. Her skirts are hitched up to reveal her knickers, of the open variety then popular, which in turn expose her bare bottom. (The revealing nature of this garment accounts for the many postcard images of recumbent ladies with their legs in the air). The frame supporting her contains a photograph of the Parisian cathedral. The pinnacle of the central dome is given a distinctly phallic meaning by its immediate context. The mildly anti-clerical meaning of the card is reinforced by the disapproving cleric whose face intrudes into the picture. Sacré Coeur has been spelled "Sacré Qoeur" by Fox. This is a verbal pun to match the visual one. The letter Q in French is pronounced "ky" which evokes the word *cul*, meaning "backside". This verbal joke stretches back at least as far as the caricaturist Argus, a contemporary of Thomas Rowlandson's. He depicted George IV cuddling his Q-ueen, and captioned the drawing "Baise mon Q---", or "Kiss my Q---". Marcel Duchamp used the joke in his celebrated reworking of the Mona Lisa (1919). He drew a moustache and beard on the lady's face and called it "L.H.O.O.Q.", which letters pronounced in French make the sentence "elle a chaud au cul", or "she has a hot backside". This was Duchamp's solution to the enigma of La Gioconda's smile.

Fox's "Hotel des Invalides", (150), mailed in 1907, is particularly interesting because you can see how it was made: the artist used a complex paper cutout collaged onto a water-coloured sky. The caption reads: "A furnished hotel for old legs that have served too long. . ." (the building was a hospital for retired servicemen). Both Cupid and the Imperial Eagle have a leg amputated and use a crutch. The naked woman covers her face presumably because she is disturbed by the mutilated couple, or is it that she cannot bear the sight of the phallic dome?

In "The Big Wheel" (151) Fox used photomontage, collage, pen and ink to portray a fairground amusement that you could enter for one franc. The spokes of the big wheel radiate from the lady's backside. They have been displaced there from the hub of the wheel, which surrounds the giant courtesan like a halo.

Fox applied his imagination to many parts of the female anatomy. In (152), "Les Halles", we see a photograph of the fruit and vegetable market juxtaposed with a portrait of one of the pretty vendors. The lady has drawn up a pile of apples in her apron. Her breasts tumble into the heap. We have come across this punning equation before. "Your apples," says a young man who is pointing to them, "are so lovely and so firm that I'd give my life to taste them."

The symbolism of "The Place de la Concorde" card (153) is really blatant. A naked girl called Madeleine has wound herself around the Luxor Obelisk. The plinth of the column is engraved with the words "The Luxor Obelisk – The concièrge remakes the beds". A policeman is about to apprehend the lady. "Have you just about finished filing down your obelisk then?" the man asks. "Vive Lépine! ! !" the girl retorts. Lépine was the Parisian Police Chief then, and le pine is a rude French word with an obvious meaning. As good as her word, Madeleine is about to lower her hind parts onto the gendarme's strategically placed truncheon.

The last in our collection of Fox's Parisian Curiosities depicts "The Maternity Hospital" (154). Above a photograph of the hospital a clown in a pointed hat gestures toward a girl holding a drawer in which an obscene little Punch sits. The clown is saying to the mother, "you've got your drawer well filled". The drawer is an obvious symbol for her womb. In fact it is a double entendre in which the function of a drawer, a box meant to safeguard things, is related to the function of a womb, a chamber for safeguarding a foetus. Double entendre is the special name given to erotic double meaning. In double meaning the two things encapsulated in one thing are related by function. In the pun, on the other hand, there is no rational link like this, but an accidental, irrational one regulated by similarities in shape. Fox's card has a macabre sense of humour. The implication is that the phallic-hatted clown is the ugly father of this even uglier, and older, son.

The First World War saw a barrage of naughty postcards, many of an unmistakable and hilarious symbolism. "Guns!... Ammo!" (see the colour plates) depicts a *poilu* rushing into the boudoir of his beloved. In his hand he has a shell. "I'm bringing you a 75", he says, referring not only to the millimetre gauge of the projectile. "And, I," says his lover, proffering her breasts, "offer you grenades!" The wartime context encouraged a whole new series of punning equations. Instead of apples, breasts might equal grenades; instead of a cathedral dome a cannon shell might stand for a phallus.

Another coloured card depicts "The Soldier's Favourite Fruits". In erotic matters the postcard artists and the people who sent postcards developed their own subtle system of signs, a genuine folk-semiology. Cards were designed and sent "in all 'languages'. In the language of flowers (highly expressive!). In stamp language. The language of eyes and handkerchiefs. In moustache language. The language of the shirt. The new language of the heart. The language of the shoe, of the umbrella, of colours, and so on" (Lauterbach and Jakovski).

The soldier's favourite fruits were intended "for local manoeuvres". The banana is "for lovers, the sign of long and happy days". The peach, on the other hand, is "round and downy" and signifies sensual pleasure. Prunes, it is said, "are best in brandy". Figs, when not too soft, mean "those two will make love like mad!" Finally, the apricot "is the most amazing fruit! It portends passionate love." The artist has emphasised the punning similarity between the fruits and certain parts of the human body. The peach is particularly evocative, and the banana finds itself in a telling configuration with two figs. Cards like these betray an admirable desire to eroticise everyday life, to invest innocent objects with a sexual meaning. To make them more innocent, that is.

The concept of the next (coloured) card, "How to Eat a Biscuit", goes back at least twenty years, to a drawing in *La Vie Parisienne* called "How the Ladies Eat Asparagus". The lewd pun between the long, thin biscuit and a phallus is explicit: the joke is about oragenital sex. The two lovers are depicted at the left surrounded by the traditional, innocent symbol of roses. After being shown "how to hold it"—good taste demanding the raising of the little finger—we see both sexes eating their biscuits in a variety of ways. A smiling man crunches his; a reclining lady sucks hers; another softens it by licking it. The correct way to eat the biscuit is, however, to dunk it in a glass of wine first, then shake off all the excess liquid before popping it into your mouth.

The symbolism of our remaining cards is if anything more subtle and diffuse than in the splendidly vulgar and obvious images discussed so far. Most of them avoid the well-defined rules of punning and double meaning in favour of a more allusive, ambiguous language.

100

In 1906 A. Bergeret & Cie., of Nancy, produced a series of cards around the subject of weathervanes, (155) to (157). In (155) a stocky, hourglass-waisted beauty becomes a weathercock high above a coastal town. Photomontage, collage, and drawing on the image are used to create this fanciful image. The cock, of course, is France's national symbol, and this female cock is cocking a snook.

"I am a *fin-de-siècle* weathervane," says the lady in (156). "The wind turns me and I turn heads." The scene is set in a similar town, on the seafront this time. The unlikely topographical relation between the steeple and the houses becomes even more unlikely when you consider that the church must be somewhere out to sea. And look at the wicked instrument she has in her hands.

"April breezes will be favourable" says the caption in (157). It shows a toothy maiden using her bellows to blow a swordfish weathervane towards the point of the compass that reads "Happiness". The other points are "Marriage", "Disappointment", and "Sorrow". The perspective relation between the steeple and the background is as unlikely here as in (156). These three cards, with their naive and fanciful design, make the sort of natural equations–between Woman, Wind and Sea–that characterised the more "authentic" and poetic cards in *I worship you, he said.*

J.-K. Huysman's novel *Là-Bas*, serialised in the *Echo de Paris* in 1891, really put Satanism on the map. The imagery of witchcraft found its way into the picture postcard via academic paintings like Louis Falero's "Witches Sabbath". This is the subject of the longest set in *French Undressing*, ten cards in all, (158) to (167). In (158) we see two young girls paying a visit to an old crone. Her den is sparcely furnished, a rumpled carpet, ladder, gourds, a *memento mori*, assorted jugs, and a large fireplace complete with cauldron is all there is. The crone helps the girls undress, and inspects the charms of her novitiates, (159) and (160). In (161) the coven is whisked away through time and space to a site like Stonehenge. The witches stir their pot. A vapour surrounds them. The vapour turns into a big black cloud in which the Devil's head appears (162). The two novices hide their faces and expose their bare bottoms, a time-honoured way of dealing with Beelzebub. The crone is not so easily frightened (163). In the next image (164) we are back in the place where it all began. The two naked novices are leaving via the chimney. Illustration (165) finds them on the roof. Photomontage and extensive redrawing went into this image. In (166) the two new witches have taken off on their maiden flight aboard two broomsticks. The last card (167) may not actually be part of the set–it is the only landscape proportioned card, all the others are portrait–but it provides a satisfactory ending to the story. We see four witches flying high above the smoking chimneys of the city skyline. Sacré Coeur, that noted Parisian phallic symbol, is prominent. The four witches may be one girl, photomontage making her multiple appearance possible. Someone has pencilled the numbers 1 to 9 on the cards. We think it possible, however, that he has put the cards in the wrong order. The narrative swings along just as happily if read (158) to (160), (164) to (167), (161) to (163).

A postscript to our diabolic set is (168). It shows a succubus about to come in through the window: "The more I gazed at that passionate witch's silhouette, the more her white eucharistic flesh under plaited viper tresses seemed to me to be marked with the irreparable kiss" (Jean Lorrain).

"The Actress' Dressing Room", (169) to (174), reverses the normal order of things by having a woman putting on rather than taking off her clothes. The eroticism lies in the fact that it is a man's clothing she puts on:

1. –I must look my best for tonight's dress-rehearsal. The theatre will be crowded with friends and enemies alike.
2. –Will this man's costume suit me? I wonder... but will it fire the enthusiasm of my friend?
3. –Let's hope for the best. I'll keep my best smile for him.
4. –Here's the little épée my friend's friend offered me so politely that I knew I wasn't completely indifferent to him.
5. –Well, so be it, let's go and face those bared hearts... and let's be charming, always charming, for to please one must know how to charm.
6. –Tonight I'm going to put everything into my part! But not for you, the public, for him! for my lover! For love commands through two lovely eyes–and man the slave must obey!

The "épée" given her by her lover's best friend was too short. Her lover, presumably, has a taste for being dominated by sword-wielding men who are not what they seem.

Women dressed as men, and swinging unsheathed blades around: cross-dressing is the theme of a similar series, again set in the dressing-room of a theatre, (175) to (180). The photographs purport to be of two different Parisian theatres, the Opéra and the Aiglon. The dressing rooms are identical–mirrors apart–the pictures were shot in neither one. In (176) a lady half-dressed in military uniform wields a sword. In (177) a valkyrie in tights holds a spear. The performers in these cards were also the first screen actresses. Méliès, for instance, used chorus-girls from the boulevard theatres –which these claim to be–in his films. They were the only actresses prepared to appear in them, their more talented colleagues considering cinematography (and postcards) too vulgar for words.

The same venue, this time masquerading as a bedroom, served for more Sapphic scenes in (181).

What are the two young girls with long, thin things in their grasp dreaming of in (182) and (183)?

No respectable woman smoked in 1900. Picture postcards of loose women smoking were therefore a big hit, (184) to (189). The cigarette became an erotic accessory, just like stockings, snowy white underwear and exposed thighs. This provides a good example of the function of context in giving new, symbolic meaning to things.

The oral emphasis is much more explicit in the set of the girl smoking opium, (190) to (195). The salon painter Vollet treated this subject in a picture called "Buddha's Poison", which was shown in 1910. The girl gives a totally abandoned performance. Her gymnastics remind us of an illustration in one of Professor Charcot's textbooks on hysteria. (Charcot was Freud's teacher).

The cards are exquisitely tinted (see the colour plates).

"Downstream" tells the story of Leda, the Greek goddess who made love to a swan, (196) to (200). The card is cleverly made. Leda lies behind a swathe of material which is dotted with straw simulating weeds, and crocuses. A stuffed swan, moving like a puppet in a puppet theatre, glides along the surface of the "water". Behind Leda is a painted backcloth representing a river bank. The whole image has been heavily retouched with broad horizontal strokes that suggest moving water. Painted rays of sunlight bathe the whole scene in an unnatural, splendid light. The narrative has Leda ultimately grasping the swan's phallic neck.

"Downstream" is popular postcard art at its best, in which rough and ready materials and methods have been used to transport the imagination to another idealised time and space. It doesn't matter that you can see the joins! All the better, given that the anthropologist Lévi-Strauss has observed that the spirit of the *bricoleur*, the handyman-artist who uses any available means in new, imaginative ways, characterises the best art. Forms and materials have no preordained function for the *bricoleur*, they find both according to his spur of the moment decisions. The *bricoleur* is the maker of myths. While it would be silly to claim that our postcards are always progressive in content–some of them are downright reactionary–the best of them are marked by this spirit of improvisation. In this sense they have a positive relation with the finer arts. This, perhaps, is what Rimbaud was talking about all along.

Œufs aux Choix

Contente ton désir,
Je te laisse choisir,
A loisir,
Suivant ton bon plaisir!

146

147

Le Mât
de Cocagne

Si mon bras peut atteindre
Le sac aux louis d'or,
De ce dernier effort
Je ne saurais me plaindre...

148

105

149

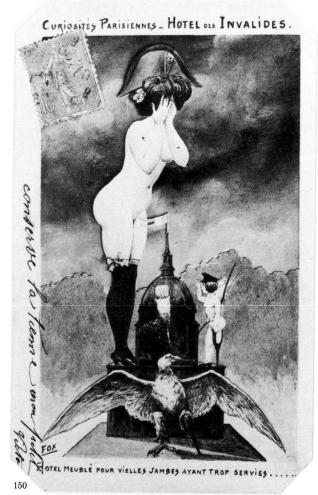

150

151

106

CURIOSITÉS PARISIENNES = PLACE DE LA CONCORDE.

OBÉLISQUE
DE
LOUQSOR
LA CONCIERGE
REFAIT
LES
MATELAS

FOX

L'AGENT = ...POUR LORS, AVEZ-VOUS BIENTÔT FINI DE LIMER VOTRE...
...BÉLISQUE...? = MADELEINE... = VIVE LÉPINE !!!.....

153

CURIOSITÉS - PARISIENNES Nº 32 = LA MATERNITÉ =

...T'AS L'TIROIR VRAIMENT BIEN......... REMPLI......

154

CURIOSITÉS - PARISIENNES Nº LES HALLES CENTRALES

VOS POMMES SONT SI BELLES ET SI VELOUTÉES QUE JE DONNERAI BIEN
MA VIE POUR Y GOÛTTER...

FOX

152

mon Clocher

t coq du village
...i comme il en a l'air ;
...'a pas peur de l'orage ;
Et son gosier chante clair.
FRÉDÉRICK.

155

La Girouette

...je suis la girouette fin-de-siècle, je tourne à tous les ve...
...is tourner toutes les têtes.

156

108

157

158

160

159

110

161

162

163

111

164

166

165

167

168

LA LOGE DE L'ACTRICE

*Il faut que je me fasse bien belle, ce soir, car c'est la
répétition générale, et la salle est comble d'amis et de jaloux.*

169

*Ce travesti m'avantagera-t-il ? peut-être !.. et réchauffera-t-il
l'enthousiasme de mon ami !..*

170

*Restons sous une impression pleine d'espérance, afin
d'avoir facilement mon plus doux sourire.*

171

Eh ! bien, soit, ayons l'audace de braver tous les cœurs...
et charmons, charmons toujours, puisque pour plaire il
faut savoir charmer !..

173

Ce soir, dans mon rôle, je vais donner toute mon âme !
ce n'est pas pour toi, public ! c'est pour lui ! pour mon
amant ! car l'amour commande par deux beaux yeux ! et
l'homme obéit en esclave !

174

Voici la petite épée que l'ami de mon ami m'a offerte, avec
une galanterie qui m'a prouvé que je ne lui étais pas
indifférente !

172

175

Loge d'Artistes. - L'Aiglon.

176

116

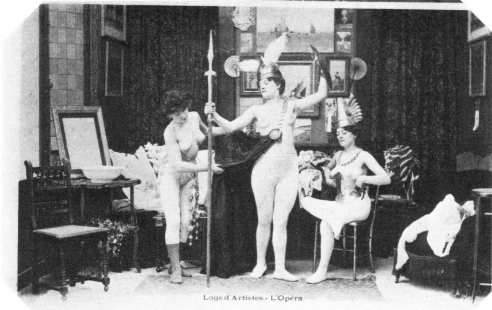

Loge d'Artistes.- L'Opéra

177

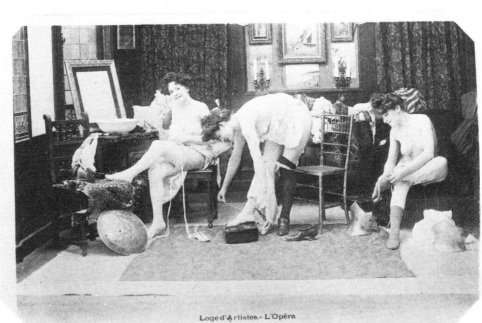

Loge d'Artistes.- L'Opéra

178

117

Loge d'Artistes.-L'Opéra

179

180

181

182

183

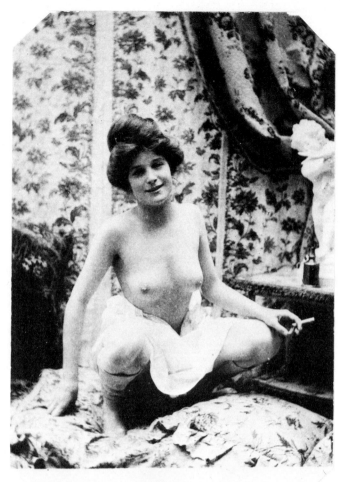

184

185

186

187

188

189

190

191

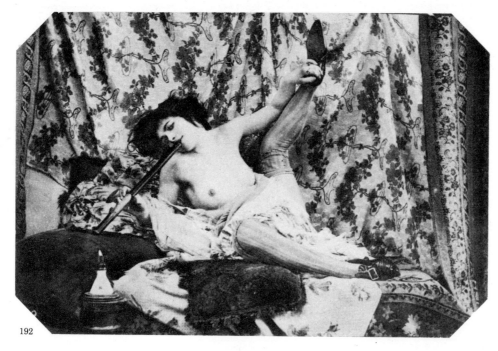

192

193

194

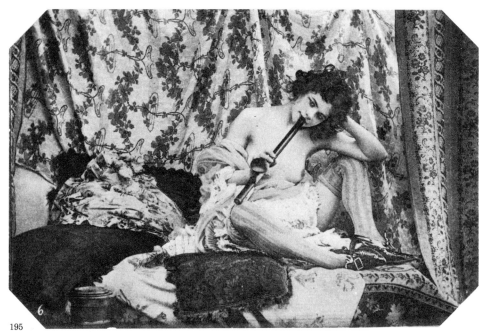

195

A VAU-L'EAU

196

197

198

199

200

5

Plain or coloured, Sir?

A postcard seller in a Berlin cafe. Cards could be bought from him and posted into the box on his back.

Postcards were generally coloured in one of two ways; by tinting or by chromolithography.

All tinting was done by hand. At first each colour was applied free-hand by a team of girls, each girl being responsible for one colour. The cost of hand-tinting hardly added to the cost of the postcard, proof, perhaps of the low wages paid and evidence, certainly, of the vast numbers of cards sold. Later on a method of hand tinting using stencils was introduced. The stencilling is most apparent when the colour is out of register with the form it is meant to tint. The quality and quantity of tinting varied. You got what you paid for, and the choice extended from totally plain, monochrome cards to the same cards completely covered in colour. Because of the transparent dyes used the colours tend to be pale rather than bold, but always luminous and lovely. Hand-tinting seems to be a characteristic of popular art. The coloured postcard has its ancestors in the hand-coloured prints of Rowlandson and his contemporaries, in the Epinal prints popular in France, and in the primitive cinema. The earliest films were hand-tinted, although usually only one or two colours were applied to the frame, which remained mainly monochrome. Around 1905 Charles Pathé introduced stencil-tinting into cinematography.

Chromolithography involves printing an image in three colours, yellow, red and blue, plus black. The colour plates in *French Undressing* were printed by this process. Its development brought pin-up artists like Hérouard, Millière and Kirchner to the picture postcard. Their coloured drawings could be accurately printed with little or no deviation in colour. These cards are now some of the most sought after by collectors. Quite frankly we don't find them as captivating as many of the less artful kinds, by Fox or Xavier Sager, say. Genuine eroticism is always something more than merely decorative (like Kirchner is), for it relies on myth, humour, and the unexpected to make it work. The pin-up as we know it today, and which Kirchner was instrumental in creating, bears false witness as far as eroticism is concerned. Pin-up stereotypes do not serve the imagination but usually deny it.

130

CURIOSITÉS-PARISIENNES Nº 32 — LA MATERNITÉ —

...T'AS L'TIROIR VRAIMENT BIEN ...... REMPLI ......

En 1re.. ligne de l'arrière!

Rêver et se conter mille choses du cœur,
C'est le calme moment, prélude du bonheur.

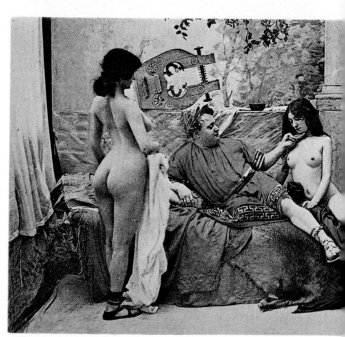

A l'Assaut

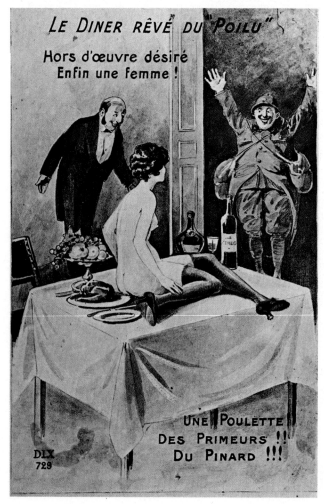

Le Diner rêvé du "Poilu"

Hors d'œuvre désiré
Enfin une femme!

Une Poulette
Des Primeurs !!!
Du Pinard !!!

DLX
729

Pour faire
l'amour
enlève
ta
capote

Les fruits
préférés
du Soldat
pour les petites manœuvres

La Banane
pour les Amoureux
est signe de
Longs Jours
Heureux

La Pêche
ronde et duvetée
est gage de Volupté

Les Prunes

Oui! ma Chérie!..
sont bien meilleures
à l'Eau-de-Vie...

Les Figues
Pas trop molles
veulent dire:
« Aimeront comme des Petites Folles! »

L'Abricot
est le Fruit le plus Épatant!
il est présage
d'Amour Ardent!

1917

LE PAPILLON

Select Bibliography

Louis Aragon, *Paris Peasant*, Jonathan Cape, London, 1971.

Richard Carline, *Pictures in the Post*, revised edition, Gordon Fraser, London, 1971.

Jean Cocteau, *Paris Album 1900–1914*, W. H. Allen, London, 1956.

Havelock Ellis, "Erotic Symbolism", in *Studies in the Psychology of Sex*, vol. II, Random House, New York, 1936.

Paul Eluard, "Les Plus Belles Cartes Postales", in *Minotaure*, no. 3–4, Paris, December 1933.

Edouard Fuchs, *L'Elément érotique dans la caricature*, C. W. Stern, Vienna, 1906.

Paul Hammond, *Marvellous Méliès*, Gordon Fraser, London, 1974.

C. W. Hill, *Discovering Picture Postcards*, Shire Publications, Tring, 1970.

Tonie & Valmai Holt, *Picture Postcards of the Golden Age. A Collector's Guide*, MacGibbon & Kee, London, 1971.

William M. Ivins, *Prints and Visual Communication*, Routledge & Kegan Paul, London, 1953.

Anatole Jakovski, *Eros du dimanche*, J.-J. Pauvert, Paris, 1964.

Philippe Jullian, *Dreamers of Decadence*, second edition, Phaidon Press, London, 1974.

Ado Kyrou, *L'Age d'or de la carte postale*, André Balland, Paris, 1966.

Carl Lauterbach & Anatole Jakovski, *A Picture Postcard Album*, Thames & Hudson, London, 1961.

J.-M. Lo Duca, *A History of Eroticism*, Rodney Books, London, 1961.

Erik Nørgaard, *With Love. The Erotic Postcard*, MacGibbon & Kee, London, 1969.

Romi, *Mythologie du sein*, J.-J. Pauvert, Paris, 1965.

Aaron Scharf, *Art and Photography*, revised edition, Penguin Books, Harmondsworth, 1974.

Roger Shattuck, *The Banquet Years*, revised edition, Jonathan Cape, London, 1969.

Patrick Waldberg, *Eros Modern 'Style*, J.-J. Pauvert, Paris, 1964.